Teachers' notes

The activities in this book are designed to support the non-specialist teacher deliver pupils' statutory IT entitlement. While there is no intention to elevate the skills-based approach to IT, it is proposed that pupils need opportunities within the curriculum to develop the necessary skills to fulfil the requirements laid down in the National Curriculum. It is only at this point that pupils can realistically integrate IT within all other subject areas. In other words IT is a set of skills which, when mastered, can be turned into powerful tools for learning.

Aims of this book

The aims of this book are:
- to support the non-specialist teacher;
- to develop word processing skills;
- to develop basic desktop publishing skills;
- to develop basic computer graphics skills;
- to develop independent learning strategies;
- to provide activities set within meaningful contexts.

Teacher-prepared files

When keying in text, or preparing any file for the whole class to use, it is a good idea to save it under a **'master filename'** on the hard disk (making a copy on a floppy disk for added security) and instruct pupils to re-save it on to their own floppy disk using a **different** filename. This will leave your original file unchanged and ready for new pupils. Files that you will need to set up in advance in order for the children to access during the lesson are: Editing text; Justification; Copy and paste; Cut and paste; Spell check.

Organisation

A whole class discussion before the activities are given to pupils is a good starting point. The activities themselves often require some preparation time at the desk. This preparation should not be underestimated and pupils' haste to 'get to the computer' should be discouraged. Good preparation will avoid time wasting at the computer which is important when the computer:pupil ratio in most classes is considered. While experimentation at the computer can be a good thing, and indeed one of the advantages of computers is the ease and speed with which this can be done, it is important to avoid mindless pondering. A good preparation tip for DTP is a 'Fonts and Clipart' book, consisting of printouts of the different fonts and clipart available, together with their name and location. This can be laminated or put into plastic covers and kept in ring binders. The clipart could be categorised to make finding the right picture easier and quicker. Thus, when planning work, pupils can list a few possible choices rather than experimenting at the computer cold.

Recording progr

By Key Stage 2, pupils should have sufficient work to justify having their own disk or at least sharing one. These should be kept in school at all times to avoid the problem of viruses. To avoid confusion at a later date the disks should also be accompanied by a list of the files, together with a brief description of what they contain and the date when the work was done. Printouts of all work are not necessary. However, each pupil or groups of pupils could be given a folder for selected examples that may be used for individual pupil portfolios.

Notes on individual activities

Page 5: Entering text

Key skills: Keying in text; knowledge and demonstration of appropriate use of shift and caps lock keys; saving to disk and printing.
The task: Children key in the two paragraphs as they appear on the worksheet. They may make their own choice of font and size. Encourage the children to save their work at short intervals, for example every five minutes, as this reduces the chances of losing a large chunk of work. The reminders at the top of the sheet serve to guide the pupils and may be focused on when introducing the task.

Page 6: Editing text

Key skills: Editing text, using the arrow keys or the mouse to move around the text.
The task: Pupils are first asked to correct the text on the sheet, using their own symbols. These should be kept simple and almost be self-explanatory. The children then correct the passage on screen.

Page 7: Justification

Key skills: To demonstrate knowledge and proper use of alignment tools.
The task: The children will need to be familiar with the layout of a formal letter (depending on the experiences of the class this may need to be addressed first). Encourage the children's replies to be as imaginative as possible.

Page 8: A diamont

Key skills: Drafting and editing using a word processor; demonstrating knowledge and use of the thesaurus and centring tools.
The task: Following the example given, pupils should attempt to write a diamont poem of their own. They should be instructed to start work at the computer without having previously done any rough

drafts. In this way they will be made aware of the editing advantages of a word processor. Encourage children to experiment with different vocabulary, changing the word order to see which works best. Suggest they use the thesaurus to help them find alternative words which they may not have thought of. While such activities may seem daunting manually, the word processor offers an easier method. The shape of the poem is crucial and the diamond shape is easily achieved using the centring tool. Withhold this information at the start if you wish to make it more of a problem-solving activity.

Page 9: Dinner table

Key skills: Organising text into a table.
The task: Children need to plan a suitable table to present the information provided. The information must be laid out accurately and sensibly but encourage the children to experiment with layout. Hopefully, the class will provide different layouts all of which work. Remind children to put the grid lines in as these are not usually automatically selected. Further formatting of text should also be encouraged. For example, the children could embolden the days of the week to make them stand out or enlarge the title text.

Page 10: Copy and paste

Key skills: To demonstrate knowledge and use of copy and paste command; highlighting text.
The task: When an object (text or graphic) is electronically copied, a replica is temporarily stored onto what is known as the clipboard (a small amount of memory set aside for this job). The object will remain there until it is pasted onto a document or replaced by another. When an object is copied, the original remains untouched. For the task, pupils will first need to manually insert the correct words and then using the prepared teacher file 'COPY', complete the same task electronically.

Page 11: Cut and paste

Key skills: To demonstrate knowledge and use of the cut and paste commands; highlighting text.
The task: When text or graphics are electronically cut they are removed from their original position and temporarily stored onto the clipboard. The object will remain there until it is pasted onto a document or replaced by another. Pupils have to find the pairs of words that need to be rearranged. They first do this manually and then electronically on the computer, using a prepared file called 'CUT'.

Page 12: Spell check

Key skills: To demonstrate knowledge and proper use of the spell check.
The task: This task aims to show pupils that while the spell check facility is a useful tool it is not a magic wand! The computer's inability to think for itself is a big consideration and when words have been spelled incorrectly only suggestions of possible corrections are listed. When two correctly spelled words have not been separated by a space they will be picked up as one word by the computer. Any word not included in the spell check's dictionary will be identified as a possible error. Many spell checks do not include names. In cases where correctly spelled words are identified the IGNORE option should be chosen.

Page 13: Thesaurus

Key skills: To demonstrate effective use of the thesaurus facility.
The task: This task requires pupils to make a 'thought' input themselves when using the thesaurus. Children will need to understand the terms 'synonym' and 'antonym'. Like the spell check, the thesaurus must be seen as a tool. Changes should only be made if they are suitable. When using the thesaurus, pupils will need to understand that the computer is not aware of the context of the chosen words. In the text, the word 'cold', for example, is an adjective but it can be used as a noun. Pupils need to identify the meaning of their words before an appropriate synonym or antonym can be found.

Graphics

Page 14: Desktop publishing

Key skills: To demonstrate knowledge and understanding of the electronic processes involved in simple desktop publishing.
The task: This activity aims to show that the processes involved in desktop publishing have not changed with the introduction of computers although the methods have. 1. Copy 2. Cut 3. Paste 4. Word processing 5. Importing graphic.

Page 15: Resize and crop

Key skills: To demonstrate knowledge and understanding of the resizing and cropping tools available in graphic and DTP programs.
The task: Following the example given, and using the grids provided, children are asked to resize the original pictures. They must then state whether they have been enlarged or reduced. You may need to explain the principle of cropping: that it allows a person to select a particular part of the drawing or illustration and use just that part by literally 'cutting off' or cropping the rest. The box for cropping the picture is left blank and pupils are required to make a rough sketch. The cropped picture should not, however, be enlarged. The example shows only the head of the robot as the rest has been cropped; the head does not fill the space and remains the same size as the original. In their experimentation, pupils may investigate all the possibilities of resizing and cropping, for example only part of a picture may be required. The rest would then be cropped and the section chosen enlarged. Alternatively, a small

background object in a picture could become the focus. Explain that if an enlarged close-up of part of a picture is required, resizing first and then cropping is the easiest way to do this.

Page 16: Cropped flags

Key skills: To demonstrate ability to crop a piece of clipart.
The task: Clipart pictures of flags are quite common in many DTP and graphics programs. Cropping allows pupils to change a picture by literally eliminating parts that the designer does not wish to use. When skills become more developed it is possible to select elements from different pictures and bring them together to form what may be a more appropriate picture. When creating the half and half flags, care must be taken with proportions. Both flags need to be the same size and cropped evenly. Some pupils may find the rulers helpful.

Page 17: Tangram

Key skills: To demonstrate use of straight line tool.
The task: Pupils are introduced to tangram puzzles in the first part of the sheet. When creating their own tangram they may choose a different shape to create. When dividing the shape they must make sure the different parts do not overlap. To ensure accuracy, the magnifying tool may be helpful.

Page 18: Impressionism

Key skills: To develop the use of the spray paint tool found in most graphics programs.
The task: Provide examples of Impressionist paintings, such as postcards, to enable pupils to appreciate the non-exact style. Children are asked to create their own Impressionist picture, but they may prefer to 'copy' part of the painting shown to them in class or take different aspects and simply mimic the style. In addition to experimenting with the spray tool, pupils will also need to think about the colours they choose in order to achieve the 'look'. To finish off, pupils may like to sign their masterpiece in black ink (handwritten, of course!)

Page 19: Logos

Key skills: Developing the use of tools found in a graphics program, including magnifying facility.
The task: Pupils are asked to list and study some commercial logos. (You may wish to introduce this topic before the lesson and ask the children to bring some examples of logos to the class with them.) Popular drinks and sports logos will be the obvious ones but there are many more, such as the school's logo and company logos. The key to a good logo is usually simplicity. Ask the children to make comparisons between the various logos they have thought of, noting any similarities. When pupils choose a logo to copy, they should be encouraged to use the magnifying tool to deal with detail. Copying fonts will prove difficult but they may decide to

choose the nearest ones and make the necessary changes themselves, using the tools available to them to add lines, rub parts out, and so on.

Page 20: Wrapping paper

Key skills: Developing knowledge and use of tools found in a graphics program; developing copy and paste skills; developing a sense of audience.
The task: Explain to the children that when designing their wrapping paper they will need to consider their audience. Wrapping paper for a christening gift, for example, will be different from Christmas wrapping paper. The preparation task at their desks should be completed carefully: only when this has been approved should pupils move to the computer. The preparation work, however, is only a guide and changes at the computer are expected.

Page 21: Picture story

Key skills: Creating simple pictures in a graphics program; importing pictures into a DTP program.
The task: Pupils need to read the story and fill in the blanks with the correct words. Some of the pictures are direct representations of the words, for example 'dress', but others are not, such as 'thunder' for 'thundered' and the picture of a bellows for 'bellowed'. The more able pupils should be encouraged to think more laterally as opposed to literally. When creating the pictures, pupils should keep them simple and save them as separate files for importing into their DTP publication or word-processing file later. The ability to resize pictures will prove useful when inserting pictures.

Page 22: Rangoli patterns

Key skills: Using tools in graphics program to produce a symmetrical pattern.
The task: The task is based on traditional Indian Rangoli patterns. The main feature of these patterns is that they are symmetrical. When colouring the pattern, pupils need to colour it symmetrically, a point they must keep in mind when creating their own Rangoli patterns.

Page 23: Mosaic pictures

Key skills: Choosing the appropriate tool in a graphics program to achieve a desired effect.
The task: Pupils create a mosaic picture or design. The mosaic design is the easiest to achieve although pictures, when kept simple, are just as easily produced. A specific tool is not suggested in this activity. Various options should be tried and tested. A helpful hint is for pupils to draw solid guidelines and then to rub these out when not needed.

Design and DTP

Page 24: Designing a menu

Key skills: To practise keying in text into text frames; to demonstrate an understanding behind the concept of frames and show skills of manipulation, including moving and resizing.

The task: Pupils need to design a suitable layout for a restaurant menu. The design stage at the desk needs to be emphasised, although amendments at the computer are inevitable and indeed desirable. The computer's ability to make changes quickly and to show a variety of styles/colours and so on, is one of the main reasons it is an excellent *tool* for designing.

Page 25: Birthday invitation

Key skills: Planning and designing for a particular purpose and audience.

The task: Show the class different types of birthday cards: humorous, modern, comical, floral, those aimed at young and old. Ask the class to come to a consensus about who the cards are aimed at, either children, teenagers, adults or elderly. What factors do designers have to take into account when creating cards? The task involves the pupils taking on board such factors in their own designing work.

Page 26: Class news sheet

Key skills: Designing a page layout for a class news sheet; defining margins and columns.

The task: Examples of newspapers should be the focus of an introductory class discussion. Points to consider should include style and size of typeface, as well as headlines and body text, and the different purposes these are used for. The language of advertising and different styles of writing, particularly report writing, should also be examined. In groups, pupils need to plan, research, design and print a class news sheet.

Page 27: Letter-headed paper

Key skills: Use and manipulation of text boxes; importing graphic into publication; use of frames and borders.

The task: Obtain some examples of printed letter-heads and show these to the children. Pupils are then asked to design letter-headed paper for a famous person based on his or her personality/achievements, and so on. Graphics can be created in separate art programs and imported if appropriate clipart is not available. Pupils can also be introduced to frames and borders.

Page 28: Getting the message across

Key skills: To appreciate the concept of white space in the designing process of a poster.

The task: Several design errors make the poster less powerful than it could be. When pupils first discover the exciting design tools available to them there is the danger of over-using them. The following design errors should be pointed out: over-use of borders distracting from the message, font style and size inappropriate, all the text is inappropriately small, except the word 'Dark' which

may be emphasising the wrong point. The text is also too wordy, the pictures are totally irrelevant and yellow lettering on a white background makes the message difficult to read. In general, the poster lacks force. Introduce pupils to the concept of white space which is just what its name suggests. Leaving spaces between text – and pupils will have to experiment with where and how much – the poster can become far more powerful.

Page 29: Spot the difference

Key skills: Cut and pasting between programs, using simple graphics tools to edit picture; planning, designing and creating a suitable page layout for a spot the difference activity sheet.

The task: Children are required to work with two separate programs and cut and paste between them. Encourage them to think of why the copy command was used instead of importing the picture twice which may seem an easier option (because it ensures both pictures are the same size/proportion). As usual, the same design questions need to be considered. A design checklist could be drawn up by groups and used when attempting such tasks.

Page 30: Design a word search

Key skills: Use of table tool to create word search grid; entering data into individual cells.

The task: Pupils first plan and then create a word search. The grid can be easily created using the table tool. Entering data into the cells can be tricky at first and can be done using the arrow keys or mouse. Before any planning, however, pupils need to decide on a topic and the question of audience will again be appropriate. A word search on food can be designed for all, but the words must suit the age-group.

Page 31: Euromoney

Key skills: Designing for a purpose; choosing appropriate software to create design.

The task: Provide a selection of paper currency from various countries. Pupils need to think about the common features of paper money and incorporate these into a design that would be relevant for all European countries. Certain issues, such as language, will need to be resolved.

Page 32: An information leaflet

Key skills: Designing for a purpose and a specific audience; setting up page layout with columns.

The task: The example leaflet shown is a good example, and any features which the children do not like are down to personal preferences (all designers have these). Children need to undertake a lot of planning before actually producing their publication on the computer. A type of program is not specified and pupils should choose a DTP program: those that opt for a word processor will soon find it limiting. Pupils should not copy the design or layout of the leaflet in the example.

Entering text

✳ Key in the story in the box below.

✳ Remember the following points:
- Key in single capital letters using the shift key.
- Never key in the letter o if you really want zero!
- Remember some keys have two symbols. For example, the £ sign and the number 3 are found on the same key.
- Use the shift key for the £ sign.

When Jenny woke up in the morning she knew it was going to be a busy day. Today was Helen's last day at school before she moved to London. Helen was Jenny's best friend. "It's time to get up," shouted Jenny's mother. "I'm up already," replied Jenny. In no time at all Jenny was washed, dressed and ready for her breakfast. A plate of scrambled eggs and toast lay on the table waiting for her. "Thanks Mum, I'll need a good breakfast today, especially with all the organising still to do," she said.

After breakfast, Jenny headed straight to her bedroom. She knelt down and pulled out a small box from under her bed. It had a label on it that read SURPRISE. Opening the box, she took out a shiny silver tin and emptied the contents on to her bed. Soon the bed was covered in coins. Very slowly, Jenny started to count them. The money was for a surprise she had planned for Helen. Jenny organised the money into neat piles and to her surprise and great delight found she had collected £10.45.

✳ Finish off the story. What might the surprise be?
- Now carry out a spell check.
- Save your work to disk.
- Print out one copy.

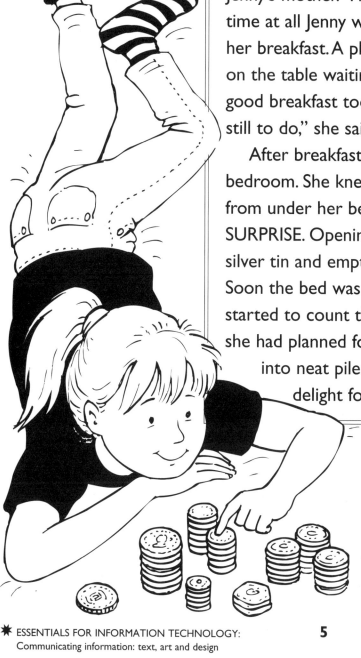

Editing text

At your desk
✴ Read the text on the right and mark the corrections using appropriate symbols.

it wass andy's firstday at his new school and everything seemed strange. It evven smelled strange. andy felt like running hhome to his mum but he knew she woould only bring himstraight back. "You must be Andy" said a tall woman who looked at andy with smiling eyes. yes" said Andy" He wanted to say as little as possiblehoping he would just fade into the background. "classsix stopp what youre doing and look this way". Andy felt his face turn a deep red and he could actually feel theheat radiating fromhis face.

What symbols did you use? In the space below sketch your symbols and explain what they mean.

At the computer
✴ Open the file called 'EDIT'.
• Save it your floppy disk using a different file name.
• Without deleting whole words, correct the text and save the changes.
• Finish off the story.
• Give your story an appropriate title.
• Print out one copy.

Justification

Justification refers to the alignment of your text.

At your desk

Look at the page layout shown on the right and note down how the text has been aligned.

The text above has been fully justified. Look at it carefully and write down what you notice.

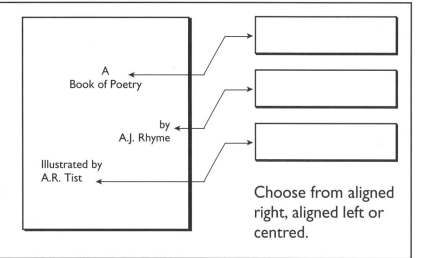

A
Book of Poetry

by
A.J. Rhyme

Illustrated by
A.R. Tist

Choose from aligned right, aligned left or centred.

The ability to align text in the above ways is very useful when writing letters. Letters have a set layout which can be achieved quickly using alignment.

✳ Look at this letter. You will notice that the layout is incorrect.

At the computer
✳ Open the file called 'LETTER'.
• Save it to your own floppy disk using a different file name.
• Correct the alignment (remember to highlight the text first).
• Write a reply to the Queen.
• Print out one copy of each letter.

The Wicked Queen
Queen's Palace
Royaldom
21 August 1998

To The Manager
Mirrors R Us
Reflection Avenue
Glassdom

Dear Mr Lines
I am writing to complain about the mirror I bought from you six months ago. For six months it worked wonderfully, but last week when I asked it 'Who was the fairest of them all?' it replied Snow White! Obviously the mirror is faulty. Please send me a replacement as soon as possible.

Yours sincerely
The Wicked Queen

✱ Name _____

A diamont

Below is an example and explanation of a diamont poem.
It consists of seven lines with a predetermined number of words for
each and has a diamond shape.

your topic

description
of topic

Wasp

annoying dangerous

actions of topic

buzzing flying hissing

further
description

wary watchful busy natural

gliding posing floating

actions of
opposite topic

beautiful colour

description of
opposite topic

butterfly

your opposite topic

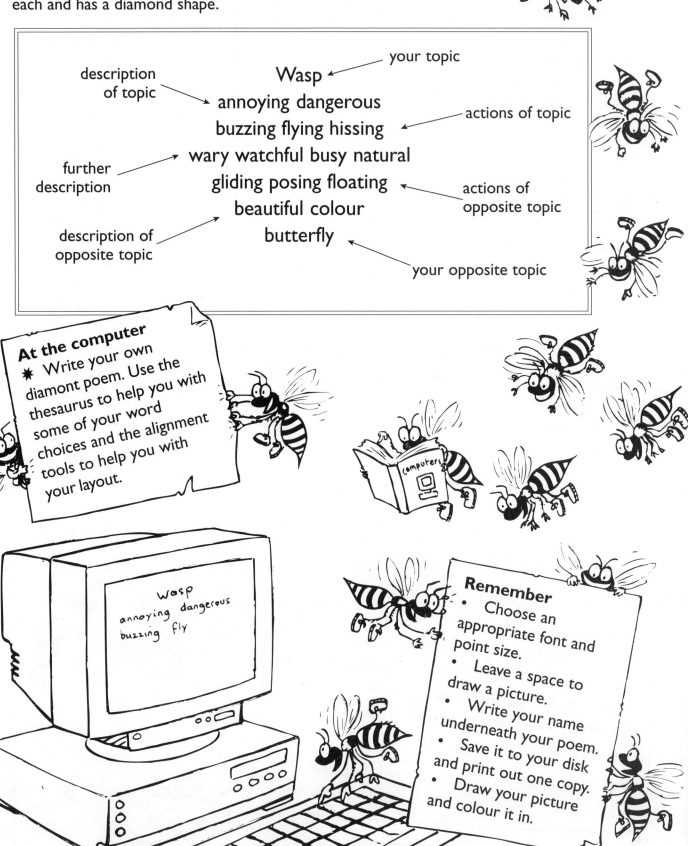

At the computer
✱ Write your own diamont poem. Use the thesaurus to help you with some of your word choices and the alignment tools to help you with your layout.

Wasp
annoying dangerous
buzzing fly

Remember
• Choose an appropriate font and point size.
• Leave a space to draw a picture.
• Write your name underneath your poem.
• Save it to your disk and print out one copy.
• Draw your picture and colour it in.

 Name _____

Dinner table

The school cook has written the school menu down very quickly on a piece of notepaper.

✳ Using a word processor, organise the information into a table so that it is much easier to read. Plan your table in the space below.

Mon   Main   Dessert
       Chicken   Jelly

Tues   Main Lamb Dessert
                   Chocolate cake

Wed   Cheese   fruit salad
       flan

Thurs Chicken pie Cream
                    buns
Fri   fish   doughnuts

Number of columns _____

Number of rows _____

Copy and paste

Word processing programs offer many advantages. They allow you to key in _____, _____ your text, _____ your text on to disk and lastly _____ your text. You can choose different _____ from fancy to plain, make these _____ or _____, _____ words, and even have your text in _____.

Best of all, you never have to rewrite (or re-enter) any of your text. Just change the parts you want to. Forgotten to include something after paragraph 1? Don't worry. Use your _____ _____ or _____ to position your cursor in the correct place and start keying in. If you decide that you do not want paragraph 4, that's fine, _____ it and press the _____ key. If you think paragraph 1 would really be better at the end, no problem, highlight it and then simply _____ and _____ it (electronically of course).

Word bank

text	print	italic
edit	paste	colour
cut	fonts	underline
save	highlight	arrow keys
delete	bold	mouse

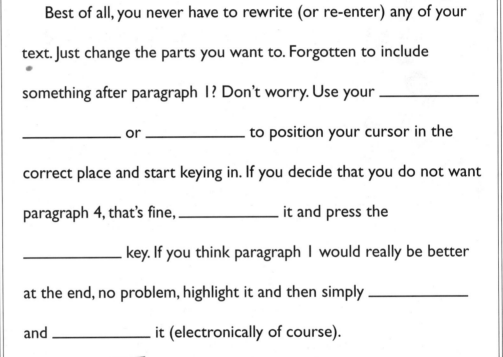

Cut and paste

At your desk
✻ Read the sentences opposite and indicate which two words have been placed the wrong way round. The first one has been done for you.

1. A computer keyboard has keys some that a typewriter does not.

2. Whenever you want to make a change you highlight must it first.

3. The point size of your characters how indicates big or small they are.

4. Spell checks only suggestions offer.

5. Computer menus not do tell you what's for dinner.

6. When you save to disk you are making a of copy your work.

7. An icon is a small picture represents that a computer command.

8. Point, click, double click and drag are all mouse-actions related.

9. Scanners text, transfer pictures or any type of diagram from a page onto the screen of your monitor.

10. Modems let communicate computers to each other using telephone lines.

At the computer
✻ Open the file called 'CUT'.
• Save it to your floppy disk using a different file name.
• You will see sentences 1–10 without the corrections. Reorder the words by using the cut and paste command.
Why would it not be appropriate to use the copy and paste commands?

_____

_____

_____

• Choose one of the sentences and turn it into a computer fact for display on a wall. Make changes to the font style, size and colour.

Spell check

At your desk

✳ Study the text in the box below carefully. Using coloured crayons, mark the mistakes you think the computer's spell check will pick up. Use the colour code to help you distinguish why the word has been pointed out by the computer.

Red	Spelling mistake
Blue	Missed space
Green	Name

Example

Missed space

Name

It was abright but breezy day when (Topsy)(wokke) up the next morning.

Spelling error

It was a beutiful day when Pinocchio decidedto venture out. He was looking forward to playying with all his new friends. He did not fee guiltie about sneeking out without permission. Pinocchio just felt very excited. After walking for about ten minites, Pinocchio came across something that caughthis eye. Everyone was having grate fun and he wanted to join in two.

✳ Count up the number of words you have marked.

How many spelling mistakes did you circle? ☐

How many missed spaces did you mark? ☐

How many names did you circle? ☐

At the computer

✳ Open the file called 'SPELL'.

• Save it to your floppy disk using a different file name.

• Carry out a spell check.

Were there any errors the computer did not pick up that you did? Can you think of a reason why?

_____

_____

Thesaurus

It was a bitterly (cold) day when Hanif decided to venture out into the High Street. Hanif was a (courteous) boy and the pushing and shoving that took place (displeased) him. Today, however, Hanif was feeling (brave) and (determined.) He clutched his pocket in which he had seven weeks' pocket-money. He had been saving it for a special present for his mother's birthday. Hanif approached the shop (cautiously.) When inside he saw a (short,) (stout) man standing next to the display that he was headed for. Hanif considered his purchase for the last time and then decided to ask for (assistance.)

✳ Key in the text as you see it.
• Carry out a spell check.
• Highlight each word that has been circled.
• Taking each one in turn, go to the thesaurus. List up to four synonyms the computer suggests. Decide if any of these words would improve the text. Change the word if appropriate.

Cold _____

Courteous _____

Displeased _____

Brave _____

Determined _____

Cautiously _____

Short _____

Stout _____

Assistance _____

What suggestions other than synonyms does the thesaurus give?

_____

Desktop publishing

✳ Look at the picture below. It shows a group of children designing a poster.
Fill in the boxes with the computerised method of performing the same task.

CUT   WORD PROCESSING   COPY   PASTE   IMPORTING GRAPHIC

✳ On a separate piece of paper, list the advantages of computerised desktop publishing.

Resize and crop

When working with pictures, a good graphics or desktop publishing program (DTP) will let you resize or crop your original picture. Look at the example on the right and see how the original has been resized or cropped.

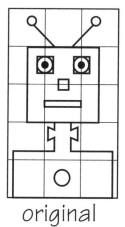 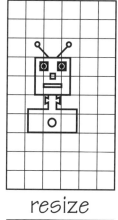 

original   resize   crop

At your desk
✳ In the same way, resize and crop the pictures below.

 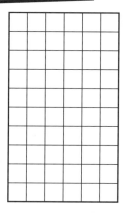 

original

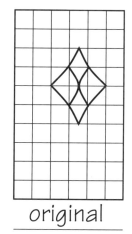 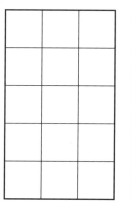 

original

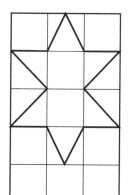 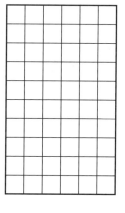 

original

At the computer
✳ Using either a graphics program or a DTP program, experiment at resizing and cropping some clipart pictures.
• Give one example when you would need to resize a picture.

_____

• Give one example when you would need to crop a picture.

_____

 Name _____

Cropped flags

At your desk
✳ Look carefully at the flag below.
What do you notice?

It is a flag made from two half flags.
The top part is the top half of the Canadian flag and the bottom part is the bottom half of the American flag.

✳ Find out the colours of the above two flags and colour them in appropriately.

At the computer
✳ Using a graphics program, make up half and half flag puzzles for your friends to work out. If you have time, import these in to a DTP program. Use your flag puzzles to make an activity sheet.
To do this you will need:
• Clipart images of flags.
• A program that will allow you to crop your image.

Remember
• Both flags need to be the same size.
• When cropping, you must crop the bottom half of one flag and the top half of the other.
• Use the ruler tool if available to help you size both halves.
• Save your work to disk.
• Print out one copy.

Tangram

A tangram is an old Chinese puzzle.

At your desk
✳ Look at the one on the right.
The six pieces together form a square but when rearranged they can form many different shapes.

✳ Carefully cut along the lines and rearrange the six pieces to form a different shape to the one shown. Use all the shapes, making sure they do not overlap.

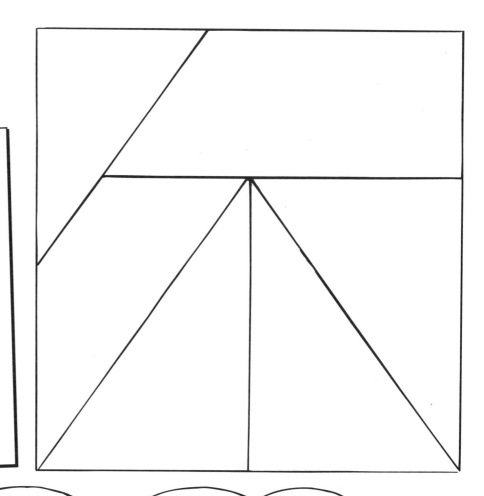

At the computer
✳ Using a graphics program, draw a shape using one of the shape tools provided.
• Now using the straight line tool, divide the shape into at least five pieces.
• Print out your tangram.
• Cut along the lines and make a design.
• When you are happy with the result, carefully stick the pieces onto a sheet of coloured paper or card.

Impressionism

Impressionism was a style of painting popular at the end of the nineteenth century. French artists, in particular, took up this unique style of painting.

At your desk
✷ Study closely some examples of Impressionist paintings, then answer the following questions.

Do you think Impressionist artists were concerned at portraying detailed images?

_____

How did Impressionist artists use colour in their paintings?

_____

_____

Do you think Impressionist art is best appreciated close-up or from a distance?

_____

Do you think everyone sees the same picture in an Impressionist painting?

_____

_____

_____

At the computer
✷ Using the spray tool in a graphics program, create a picture in an Impressionist style.
• Print out one copy.

✷ Using either a CD-ROM or the Internet, carry out some research on Claude Monet or another Impressionist artist.

Logos

Commercial logos are found everywhere and are used to sell many different products. Think of how popular sports logos are.

At your desk
✻ Make a list opposite of some popular brand names that have logos.

At the computer
✻ Choose your favourite logo. Using the magnifying tool in a graphics program to help you, try to re-create it as closely as possible.

Which part of the logo was the hardest to copy?

_____

_____

What do you think makes a good logo?

_____

_____

_____

_____

Wrapping paper

At your desk
✳ Design a small logo that will be repeated across the page to make some wrapping paper for a birthday present, for example a balloon or a birthday cake. Sketch out a few rough designs in the boxes below.

✳ Make a note of the tools you are expecting to use when creating your design on the computer.

At the computer
✳ Create your design using a graphics program and paste it repeatedly across the page.
• When creating your design, you may find it helpful to use the magnifying tool.
• Print out your work.

Picture story

There was once a woman called _____ who was married to a man named

[sun picture] [flower picture]

_____. One day when the _____ was shining, _____

[bellows picture] [eye picture]

_____ to her husband '_____, _____ want a new

[bottle picture] [waves picture]

_____,' _____ answered '_____ will have to

_____ the shop to _____ if it is open.' 'The shop is closed my

[deer picture] [stamp picture]

_____' said _____. With a huff and a puff and a _____

[feet picture] [flower picture] [storm cloud picture]

of her _____, _____ _____ off.

Can you work out what words the pictures represent?

✹ Fill them in using the spaces provided.

At your desk
✹ Plan a picture story like the one above.

At the computer
✹ Create your pictures in a graphics program. Do not be too concerned about size as you will be able to resize your pictures later.
• Save each picture separately.
• Note down the filenames.
• Now select an appropriate program that will allow you to create a picture story.
• Save your work to disk.
• Print out one copy.

Rangoli patterns

Rangoli patterns are often used to decorate floors at Divali time. They are usually created using coloured powders or special pastes made from flour, paint and water.

At your desk

✱ Look at the Rangoli pattern on the right.

What do you notice about the pattern?

_____

_____

_____

✱ Colour the Rangoli pattern so that it keeps its symmetry.

At the computer
✱ Using a graphics program, design a Rangoli pattern.

✱ Find out about the story of Lakshmi and the Lotus flowers. You might like to research the story using a CD-ROM or the Internet.

Mosaic pictures

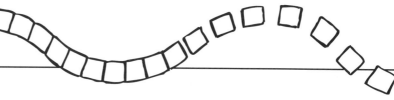

At your desk

✳ Look at the mosaics below. One is a mosaic design and the other is a mosaic picture. Both are made using small shapes positioned together closely.

✳ Using coloured crayons, colour the above mosaics.

At the computer

✳ Using a graphics program, find an appropriate tool that will help you to produce a small mosaic design or picture.

✳ Plan your work in the space below.

Designing a menu

MENU	STARTERS	MAIN COURSE	DESSERTS
Minestrone soup Garlic mushrooms Prawn cocktail	Vegetable bake Roast chicken Lasagne	Fruit fool Chocolate dream cake Lemon sorbet	

At your desk

✳ On a piece of paper, design the layout for the above menu. Think about the purpose of the menu and who will be reading it. To save time you may like to cut out the text boxes and glue them into position once you've decided on a layout. Choose appropriate fonts and indicate effects using pencil notes.

At the computer

✳ Reproduce your design on the computer using a desktop publishing program.
Did you make any changes?

_____

_____

_____

What advantages does the computer method have compared to the manual method?

_____

_____

Birthday invitation

At your desk

✳ On a piece of blank paper, plan a rough sketch of a child's 5th birthday invitation. Indicate effects using pencil notes. Remember to include the following details:

> Name of sender
> Venue
> Time
> Date
> Reason for invite
> Replying procedure

✳ Repeat the above process, this time designing an invitation for a person's 60th birthday party.

✳ Describe and explain the differences between the two invitations.

_____

_____

_____

_____

_____

At the computer
✳ Using your rough plans as guides, create your invitations using a desktop publishing program.
• Print out one copy of each.

Class news sheet

You are going to design a news sheet.
✸ In groups of five discuss the content of your news sheet.
You must include the following:

> One headline news story
> One other item of news
> At least one picture (not hand drawn)
> One small competition
> One advertisement

Decide between you who will do each of the above. Carry out some research then write up your section. Make a rough plan of your news sheet. The diagram on the right shows an example.

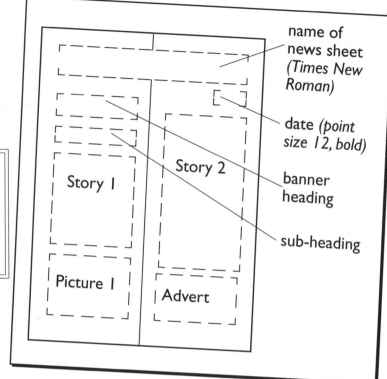

name of news sheet (*Times New Roman*)

date (*point size 12, bold*)

banner heading

sub-heading

Story 1

Story 2

Picture 1

Advert

At the computer
✸ Dividing the task between the group, create your news sheet, remembering to set up your page layout so that there are at least two columns.
• Print out one copy.

Letter-headed paper

At your desk
✴ Think of a famous person, either real or fictitious, dead or alive and describe them.

Name _____

Character _____

_____

_____

_____

_____

✴ Now, taking the above information into consideration, design some letter-headed paper for this person. Include the person's name and address (you may need to be creative for this).
✴ Choose an appropriate font and personalise the paper according to that person's character.

For example:

Name Prince Charming

Character loving
        faithful
        serious
        handsome
        caring
        romantic

Prince Charming
Lovers Walk
Lovelorn

At the computer
✴ Using a DTP program, create your personalised letter-headed paper.
• Save to your disk.
• Print out one copy.

Getting the message across

(All text is yellow on a white background.)

BE SAFE, BE SEEN

Wear reflective material at night and fluorescent material in the day.

Road safety

Always wear bright clothes that will make you easy to spot by motorists.
Never wear **DARK** clothes.

At your desk

✳ Look at the sketch of a poster above.
Do you think it has a clear message?

✳ Make a list of all the design errors you think have been made.

_____

_____

_____

_____

_____

_____

_____

Safety on ladders

At the computer
✳ Using a DTP program, redesign the above poster.
✳ Feel free to delete certain items, and if appropriate add others. Make a rough sketch before you start.

Spot the difference

At your desk
* Plan a spot the difference activity sheet. Include the following:

Title
Space for two pictures
Instructions
Space for solution

At the computer
For this task you will be using a DTP program and a graphics program.

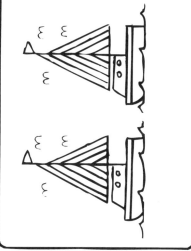

Choose from the clipart library a picture that will be the focus for the spot the difference. Place the picture onto your DTP page and size it so that it is roughly 6cm x 6cm.

Now select the picture and make a copy of it. Paste it onto your page and position it next to your original. You should now have two identical pictures.

Select one of the pictures and cut it – thus removing it from the page.

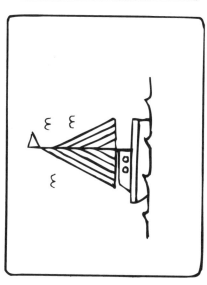 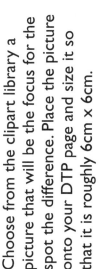

Now load your graphics program and paste the picture you cut here. Using the tools available, make six changes.

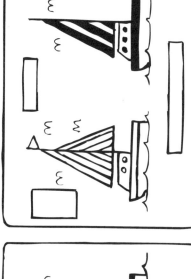 

When you have finished, cut the picture and re-paste it onto your DTP page.

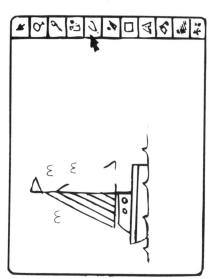

Using text boxes and other features, add the finishing touches to your activity sheet.

Design a word search

At your desk
✳ Plan a word search using the grid below.

Subject:

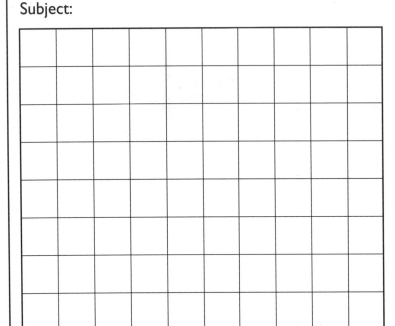

Only place your ten words into the grid at this stage.

Words:

_____

_____

_____

_____

_____

_____

_____

_____

_____

_____

word bank

At the computer
✳ Using a DTP program, design a word search activity sheet. Include the following:

Title.

Word search grid (use table tool for grid). You may now add the extra letters to hide your words.

List of words to find.

Instructions.

Appropriate illustrations – these may be clipart, scanned images or pictures produced yourself using a drawing program and imported into your publication. They may not be hand-drawn.

• Save to your disk.

• Print out one copy.

Euromoney

Every country has its own money. Though money from different countries may look different it contains similar features.

At your desk
✸ Look at paper money from several different countries and make a list of the things that are common to all.

_____

_____

_____

_____

_____

_____

✸ Imagine that you have been asked to design some new European money that all the countries of Europe will use. Plan your design below.

At the computer
✸ Using an appropriate program, re-create your design.

An information leaflet

At your desk
✸ Look at the leaflet opposite and answer the following questions.

What is the leaflet about?

_____

_____

Do you think the picture is helpful? Why?

_____

_____

Would the leaflet take you a long time to read?

_____

Do you think the leaflet is informative? _____

_____

Is there anything about the leaflet you do not like? _____

_____

How would you improve the leaflet? _____

_____

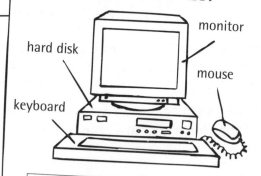

CARING FOR YOUR COMPUTER

monitor

hard disk

mouse

keyboard

NEVER eat/drink near your computer.

NEVER pull plug out, always shut down properly.

COVER your computer when it is not in use.

NEVER place your floppy disks in direct sunlight.

Caring
for your
human

At the computer
✸ Design an information leaflet about caring for a pet of your choice. Remember the following:
- Research your topic so that the information is accurate.
- Include pictures if they will help with explanations.
- Decide who your leaflet is aimed at and present your information accordingly.
- Choose fonts and colours carefully.
- Do not overdo it. Only use special effects if they will improve the leaflet.
- Save your work to disk.
- Print out your leaflet.